Officer Down

Officer Down

The Dangers Every Cop Will Face

Billy Grinslott

Billy Grinslott

Officer Down

Copyright © Billy Grinslott
All rights reserved.
ISBN: 9798510444513
Billy Grinslott

Officer Down

DEDICATION

This book is dedicated to all the great Americans, that still believe that the United States is a great place to live.

All the great Americans who still believe that we need to protect our constitution, our heritage, and our way of life.

For everyone who is struggling, a brighter future.

Billy Grinslott

Officer Down

Billy Grinslott

Officer Down

CONTENTS

Acknowledgements   i

CHAPTERS

1	Introduction	Pg 3
2	A Day on the Highway	Pg 4
3	My Experience	Pg 7
4	Handcuffs	Pg 11
5	Dangers Cops Face	Pg 19
6	Hazards Cops Face	Pg 24
7	Bad Neighborhoods	Pg 26
8	Officer Down	Pg 29
9	Racial Tensions	Pg 31
10	Cops no Cops	Pg 36
11	Dialing 911	Pg 48
12	Conclusion	Pg 50

Billy Grinslott

Officer Down

Officer Down

ACKNOWLEDGMENTS

Thanks to Dustin Michael, Devan Brandt, Kinsey Marie, Robyn Kelly, Julie Berg for all their insight and Help.

Officer Down

Officer Down

Introduction

Officer down, the dangers every cop will face. Police officers face all kinds of scrutiny, hazards, assaults, and attacks while on duty. Being a cop has become a dangerous profession and their life is on the line.

In this book, I will discuss all those topics, the good, the bad and the ugly. I will also discuss the life of a cop. What it's like to be a cop. How they are treated. What they must put up with. Along with all the hazards they face daily.

To walk in a cop's shoes, is like asking for a death sentence. Just putting on a badge makes them a target. Take a look at the dangers a cop must face every day, by reading this book.

There's a lot of controversy going on in America right now. There seems to be a lot of mixed emotions when it comes to cops. There's a lot of talk about police reform, defunding or dismantling police.

2020 will go down as one of the biggest years for chaos and uprising in our country. The death of George Floyd sparked one of the biggest uprisings in America. The issue is an all-out attack on police officers took place. Because of this, crime rates have risen significantly.

One of the issues we face right now in America is, we have some individuals and organizations that are creating chaos in our society. The problem is its disrupting the lives of the rest of us, who just want to live a peaceful life. We will get into that in a minute, I want to say a couple things first.

One thing I would like to make clear before you read the rest of this book is, I'm a brutally honest person. I must be, It's the way I was trained. I also look at both sides of an issue and don't take any animosity towards anyone's opinion.

In this book, I'm going to tell the truth, no sugar coating added. I'm going to back it up with facts. Now the first thing I want to say is, I understand human nature. I've got over 30 years' experience monitoring people's behavior.

Let's talk about human nature a little bit. Even though I'm going to back up what I say in this book with facts, there's going to be some people who do not agree with it. They are going to yell and scream, call me names, and maybe pull out the race card.

What I want to say is we are all entitled to our opinions. If we agree, great. If we disagree, let's just leave it at that. There's no reason why two people can't have different opinions and still respect each other at the end of the day. So, let's get started

A Day on The Highway

Most of us start off our day by getting up and getting ready for work. This usually involves grabbing a cup of coffee before heading out the door. We have a nice peaceful start to our day. Then the stress begins. The most stressful part of most individual's day is the drive into work.

Yah it's a lot of fun for most people dodging cars, driving as fast as possible, weaving in and out of traffic, cutting people off. Slamming on the breaks, yelling at other drivers.

When most of us get to work, after were done complaining to our coworkers about all the idiots on the road, the stress is gone. Most of us have a quiet normal day. At the end of the workday, we head home.

When we get home, we eat, spend time with the family. Turn on some tv, watch our favorite sport or tv show, read a book or whatever else makes us happy. For the most part we live quiet normal lives. We just go about our routine and do it all over again the next day.

I started off this book by talking about your drive to work. That your stress ends when you get to work. I want you to think about this during your next 8-hour workday or however long it is. You are now off the highway. But someone is still out on that highway. They most likely will be there for the next 8 hours.

That's right, it's a cop. What you had to put up with during your drive into work, they must put up with for the next 8 hours. There's a huge difference of what they are going to have to deal with on their job, compared to yours.

Eventually to end all this chaos and erratic driving, the cops are going to have to make their presence known by pulling someone over. Consider yourself lucky because you made it to work. Even though you just drove like mad man and you were in the Daytona 500.

Most cops don't pull people over for no reason. Oh boy here comes human nature. So, a cop just pulled someone over for speeding. He walks up to the car and says, do you know why I pulled you over. Ah dah, tweedily dee, tweedily dumb ahh, ahh. No officer I don't know why you pulled me over. I pulled you over for speeding, I got you doing 70 in a 55.

I wasn't speeding. It all starts with the dumb act and then a lie. Now the cop knows he's lying, he's not an idiot. So, as he asks for the guy's license and insurance.

What the cop doesn't know is he just got a hold of a bad actor. The guy starts yelling and screaming at him. Starts calling him names and accuses him of being racist.

Human nature is funny. This guy knows he was speeding and now it's all the cop's fault for pulling him over. Not only is he going to blame the cop, but he's also going to downgrade the officer while he can.

All of this out of a normal traffic stop. Now the cop hopes that this is the only way that the guy is going to overreact. That his intensions aren't worse like pulling out a gun and trying to shoot him.

Most likely this scenario is not going to turn out well for the speedster. One thing is for sure, the speedster just decided his fate, that he most likely will get a ticket because of his own actions. If the cop had any thoughts of just writing a warning, the speedster changed that outcome.

Now, you might be thinking why I started this book out this way. Here's why. The cop is just doing his job. When you were at work, did your coworkers yell at you. Did they call you names or accuse you of being racist? No, they didn't.

You wouldn't put up with that for one second at your job or anywhere else. Then what makes you think that a cop should have to put up with it, when they are just doing their job. Kind of makes sense that everyone should be treated with respect when they are at work or anywhere else for that matter.

Yet, there's some people that think they can downgrade or belittle police officers. Doesn't make any sense why someone would think this is ok, when they don't want to be treated this way. They surely would not put up with this at their job. Then why do they think a cop wants to put up with it or deserves too.

Human nature is to blame someone else for your actions. Well, it's not someone else's fault when you're doing something wrong. If you're speeding or breaking the law, just own up to it and take the punishment. The next time a cop pulls you over, thank him or her for all the crap they had to deal with to keep your community safe.

My Experience

If you want to talk about speeding, I'm the man to talk

too. I've been pulled over for moving violations at least 40 to 50 times in my life. I've owned some nice cars and I like to drive fast. Heck some of the beaters I've owned, I drove fast. I just like to drive fast.

Here's what I can tell you, for the number of times I've been pulled over, I can count on one hand the number of fines I've gotten. I've gotten out of a lot of fines. Whether you want to believe this or not, it's true. I will tell you why and how.

The last time I got pulled over, I was on my way to work. The speed limit on the highway was 65 mph and I had my cruise set at 74mph. Typically on this highway there's plenty of cops and if you keep your speed under 10 over, they don't bother you. This is typical on a lot of roads.

I'm not suggesting that you speed nor am I saying you should follow my advice. If you decide to speed that's your fault, don't blame me. My suggestion is following the speed limit and don't speed.

The next thing I notice is lights in my rearview mirror. I flip the turn signal on, and I immediately pull over as far over on the shoulder as I can get. Now you might ask why I get over as far as possible. It's to take the cop and yourself out of harm's way.

If you don't think cops take this into consideration, you are sadly mistaken. They would rather get out of a car that is off the road, then step out of one that is halfway on the highway. I've had cops ask me why I pulled over so far and my response Is. I'm concerned about your safety, my safety and everyone else's.

Here's what you need to do next. There are only 4 movements you will make and then you will sit perfectly still. Here's the movements. Place the vehicle in park, turn it off if you want too. Turn off the stereo. Roll Down the window. Place your hands on the wheel at 10 and 2 position and don't move another inch.

Here's what's happening behind you at this point. The cop is calling on his radio and waiting for response to get your information. Whether you believe it or not, he is staring at you in your vehicle while this is taking place. That's right the cop is watching every one of your movements.

Keep your hands on the wheel and do not move. Don't start digging for your wallet, insurance, or registration. If you do, the cop is probably thinking all this movement, is to hide something. Take it from me do not move, it will all work out in a minute. You will have time to dig for your stuff when the time is right.

As I'm sitting there with my hands on the wheel the cop finally walks up to the car. Remember, do not remove your hands from the wheel. The only motion you will want to make when the cop is standing next to your car, is to turn your head and look at them.

The very first words the cop says to me are, do you know why I pulled you over. My reply is for speeding, I had my cruise set at 74 mph and it's a 65mph zone and I was speeding. He replies well I clocked you at 76mph. My reply is, there may be something wrong with my speedometer. It may be off a little bit, I just put new tires on the vehicle about 2 weeks ago.

The cop looks down at my tires and says those do look new. I repeat, I just put them on a couple weeks ago. The cop says, do you have your license and insurance. I say to the officer, my wallet is in that cooler sitting in the passenger seat. Do you care if I reach in there and grab it? He says what is that cooler for anyway, do you have any alcohol or weapons in it. I said No, I'm on my way to work and it's what I keep all my stuff in.

I say it's not really a cooler, it's more like a man purse. I keep my wallet, papers, checkbook, and other belongings in it. Do you care if I get my wallet out of it? He replies no, go ahead. Now is when one hand only will come off the wheel. I take my right hand in a normal movement, reach over, open the cooler, grab the wallet, and hold it up in plain sight. Bring it over and hold it straight out in front of me.

Then I say do you care if I get my license and insurance out of it. The officer replies no, go ahead. I must use both hands to do this, so I do. After I get the cards out, I hand them to the officer and place my hands back on the wheel.

The officer looks at me a says, I don't need your registration, it came up under your name. I will be right back. He then turns and walks to his car. While he's in his car, what do you think I'm doing. Nothing, my hands are plastered on the wheel and I'm not moving one muscle.

He's in his car and he has a decision to make.

Officer Down

While he's making that decision, he's watching me. Eventually he climbs out of his car and walks back up to mine. I turn and look at him and he hands my license and insurance back and says, I'm going to let you off with a verbal warning, slow down. Just knock your speed down a little bit and you'll be fine.

My reply is, thank you very much for not giving me a ticket those things can really wreak havoc with my insurance. He says, no problem. I say have a nice day; he replies you too.

Why has this scenario worked so many times for me? First, I really do care for cops, they have a job to do and that is to keep the community safe. By getting him out of harm's way, proves that. By not moving in my car, did two things. It showed I had nothing to hide and put him at ease because he realizes this. By keeping my hands on the wheel, shows that I'm no threat to him, which also puts him at ease.

By admitting my guilt of speeding and not trying to lie to him, puts him at ease. By letting him know what I needed to do before removing my hands from the steering wheel, also puts him at ease. The point is, I did everything I could do to show the officer I was willing to work with him and I was no threat to him. This all made his job easier.

Now this may not work every time, but it has helped me get out of a lot of tickets. One thing you must know about cops is, they really don't want to ruin your day by writing a ticket. Many cops will tell you this.

In this next chapter you will realize why remaining calm and doing what you are asked to do will benefit you in the end.

Handcuffs

I've been in handcuffs twice in my life. One was just a simple case of mistaken identity. The car I was driving matched the car of a reported crime. I was pulled over, asked to get out of the car, went through the routine of raising my hands, backing up to the officers and getting handcuffed.

After the handcuffs were on, I asked the officer what it was all about. He says your car matches the description of a rape suspect we're looking for. I reply, it's not me. He replies we have a call in for the descriptions of the guy, we'll know in a minute, ok.

The call comes back, and the cop looks at me and says, you don't match the description, I apologize, let me get those cuffs off. I said thanks, I hope you catch the bastard. On my way.

This scenario could have turned out bad for me depending on my reactions. I had no clue of why I was asked to get out of my car at gunpoint and had to go through this routine. What I did know, is it's best to just follow their directions and work out the details later. I didn't get shot, I lived to see another day.

How I reacted, determines the outcome. As you will see in the next scenario, by working with the cops, saves me a lot of grief and money.

Officer Down

So, there I am going out on a Friday night driving my Mustang and cruising just as fast as I can. Here comes the red lights. So, I follow my normal routine as I explained before. I pull over, shut it down, turn off the radio, put my hands on the wheel. But something isn't right.

As I'm sitting in my car with my hands on the wheel, it's taking a long time for the cop to get out of his vehicle and come up to the window. As I'm looking in my rearview mirror, I get the answer. Coming down the highway are two more cop cars. They pull in behind the first squad car.

Eventually all three officers approach the car. One walks around the passenger side and the other two approach the driver's side. They don't have their weapons drawn, but their hands are on their weapons. Why aren't their weapons drawn, because my hands are in clear view on the wheel' I'm posing no threat.

One cop walks up to the window and asks, are you so and so. I reply yes. Is this your car, I reply, yes? He replies, do you know you have a warrant for your arrest. I reply no, I'm not aware of any warrant for my arrest. I haven't done anything illegal. What is the warrant for, I don't know, it's been called into the county it's out of and we should have an answer in a couple minutes?

I say what do you need me to do. He replies I need you to get out of the car. I reply, do you care if I open my door. He replies, is it unlocked, I say yes. He says I'll open it, ok. The door goes open.

There's only one problem at this point, my seatbelt is still on. I say can I undo my seatbelt to get out. He asks if I have any weapons in the car, no. Ok undo your seat belt and step out, so I do. I place my hands directly in front of me as I get out and present them to the officer. He grabs my left hand and says place your right hand on your head, I do. He cuffs my left hand and says turn around. I turn around and he grabs my right hand from my head and cuffs it. I'm now cuffed.

You might be asking yourself why I'm going into detail on this, remember in the last chapter when I said the best thing you can do is pose no threat. Always keep your hands in full sight. How do you think they would react if when I got out my car, I put my hands in my jacket or pockets? How do you think they would react if when he told me to turn around, If I dropped my other hand off my head? Do exactly what they tell you. Any extra movements can lead to confusion and trouble. Not to mention getting tased or shot.

You must look at it this way. They don't know what the warrant is for and they don't know what kind of character I am, they don't know what they're dealing with. They don't know if I have a weapon on me and I'm lying to them. Follow their directions precisely and do not put your hands anywhere near your body.

Everything you can do to calm the situation down, is a good thing. They are just doing their job. It doesn't do any good to have an attitude toward them or get frustrated.

They now walk me around the front of the car and ask me to stretch out over the hood of my car and frisk me. Then they tell me to sit on the hood and I do. At this point you can see everyone is relaxed. I'm telling them that I have no idea what the warrant is for. Just about then, here comes the radio call. Across the radio comes the explanation for the warrant. It's a petty warrant, a minor violation.

When I hear it, I can't believe it? I tell the cops, trust me, I took care of that 6 weeks ago. I can prove it, I've got all the paperwork and the receipts where I paid for it, I'm not lying, it's been taken care of.

They respond, either way, we still must take you to jail for the warrant and we're going to have to tow your car, we can't leave it sitting here. I say guys come on, is there anything we can work out here. How much is it for me to bail out tonight. They reply, on this charge around $400.

I reiterate that I've taken care of this and I would really appreciate it if you wouldn't tow my car. I'm going to go down to jail and bail out in probably a couple hours and I really need my car. It would be greatly appreciated if it weren't towed.

They put their heads together and come up with a plan. They are going to leave the car sit and tag it for midnight. What this means is they are going to place a tag on it not to be towed till after midnight. That way any other officer or tow truck that comes along, will leave it sit until after that time.

I thank them and say let's get this show on the road. They laugh. I then say hey I'm lucky you guys pulled me over now, rather than later. They ask why. Because I was headed to the casino to play cards and drink, later I would have been drunk. They all laugh. Whether you believe it or not, cops are normal people. They like to have fun too.

Then the cop who pulled me over says. Alright let's put you in my car and I will run you down to the station. I say hey on the way can we stop at an ATM, he chuckles and says why. My wallets got $380 in it. I just need $20 to bail out. He laughs and says, you know I can't do that. I know but it was worth a try.

On our drive to the station, we have a normal conversation. When we show up at the station, I'm expecting to be put into a holding cell. Instead, the officer walks me into a room where 3 other officers are sitting at their desks doing paperwork. He takes the handcuffs off and says, you can wait with these guys, use any of the phones to call someone and get the money you need to bail out, these guys will help you.

I thank the officer before he leaves to go back on patrol. I make my phone call and get my son & daughter to bring me the money. For the next hour, I sit and bullshit with these officers. They even offer me a sandwich and pop while I'm waiting.

Eventually the kids show up with the cash, I thank the officers for their help and bail out. Now you might be thinking, how did I get so lucky to have such a good experience. I don't think it's all luck. I think it has a lot to do with how you act and treat others.

From the very moment that officer pulled me over, I made it aware to him, that I was no threat. I respected him and did everything I was asked to do. In return, he repaid the favor and helped me out. There are always positives in everything. The cops are not to blame for the warrant, they are just doing their job. So why take it out on them. I saved $500 to $1000 that night because they didn't tow my car.

Cops are normal people. If you treat them good, they will treat you good. If you want to treat them badly, then expect to get treated the same way. You get the point.

The ending, a week later I go to court for this deal. I bring all the paperwork and the payment receipt to court. See, I didn't lie to the officers. I had already taken care of it. I present all the paperwork to the judge and it's at that point where he apologizes to me and says, there's been a clerical error here.

You took care of it, but the paperwork didn't make it into the system for some reason. I reply with, mistakes happen, we all make mistakes. The judge says once again, I'm sorry you shouldn't have gone through this. I'm going to wipe all this off your record. On the way out stop by the cashier's window and get the money back you put up for bail. Ok, thanks. Out I go.

I could have reacted completely different. I know

there's some people thinking that I should have lost my temper with the judge and gave him a piece of my mind. I should be upset with the court for not filing the paperwork correctly.

I also realize that its human nature for many people to react like this. My point is what good does it do to get your blood boiling. It's not the judge's fault, why take it out on him. Everyone makes mistakes, that's right no one is perfect.

My life has been no different than yours. I've been through some hard times, but I've also had good times. I consider myself lucky and here's why. Life can always be worse. Everyday so far, I've been lucky to be able to stand on my own two feet and do something with my life and enjoy life.

Here's how I keep grounded and have learned not to let the petty stuff bother me. I want you to think about this. Imagine that you're strapped into a wheelchair and the only way you can eat is through a straw. Someone must bathe, clothe, and change your diapers every day.

What I'm trying to say is that no matter how bad you think your life is, it can always be worse. If your lucky enough to be able to stand on your own two feet, be happy and do something good with your life. All the animosity, running around yelling and screaming, being agitated, does no good. It just makes you miserable and everyone around you.

Now I don't want to carry on too much before we get into this book, but I would like to tell you something I told my son once. My son has rolled over 3 vehicles in his life. All these happened because of weather conditions, driving too fast, and not paying attention. Luckily, he didn't get any major injuries in any of the rollovers.

After he rolled his third vehicle, I asked him if he didn't like walking around on this planet. He said what. I asked, what do you think is the worst thing that can happen to you when you roll over a vehicle.

He says I could die. I said no, when your dead, your dead, everyone else will be sad, but your dead.

The worst things that can happen is, you end up in a hospital bed with machines keeping you alive. You end up in a wheelchair crippled for the rest of your life.

How would you like to live like that? He replied, I wouldn't. Then slow down and pay attention, cause there's way worse things that can happen and there's way worse ways to spend life.

My point is, Life can always be worse. If you're lucky enough to be able to stand on two feet, make the best of it, be happy. Running around with hatred, animosity and being agitated does absolutely no good.

Dangers & Issues Cops Face

In this chapter we're going to discuss the stuff that cops must put up with when they're on duty or at their jobs. Many of the issues, assaults and attacks they deal with are uncalled for and they don't deserve to be put in this spot.

Criminals. Cops get to deal with the worst people in America. Every day when they go to work, they deal with people that are committing crimes. The problem is some of these individuals aren't committing simple crimes. Some of these criminals are hard core individuals that are capable of just about anything. When cops confront these individuals, they are most likely going to be assaulted in some form or shot at. Yet they do this to keep the community and society safe. They put their life on the line for you.

Disrespect. It's amazing how society has changed and thinks its ok to disrespect officers. Everyday police officers are disrespected when they are on duty. They are just trying to do their job of keeping your community safe and they get disrespected because of it. Amazing how everyone else demands respect in their lives and at work, but they feel its ok to disrespect others. If anything, cops deserve respect for dealing with the people and issues that you don't want too.

Discrimination. Cops face discrimination in many ways. They are discriminated against because for some reason just being a cop has become a bad thing. Belonging to a group of people that put their lives on the line to protect everyone else has become a bad thing. Cops also face discrimination and are accused of it. Every time they deal with people of a certain ethnicity, they are accused of discrimination. Most cops don't discriminate, they are about 99% accurate in their assumption that a law is being broken and the individual is at fault. Yet some people want to yell discrimination or blame the cops, because they don't want to own up to what they've done or who they are. Got to use the trump card.

Unfairness. Cops are not treated very fair. They put their lives on the line every day to make our communities a safe place to live. They have a dangerous and tough job, that most people couldn't do, or wouldn't do. Then they are treated like they are the scum of the earth. They are portrayed by some people and organizations as being the bad guys. When they are the ones protecting society from the bad guys.

Attacks. There are over 58,000 assaults against law enforcement officers each year. That's around 160 per day. How would you like to work under these conditions? Knowing when you go to work, you will most likely be assaulted. This doesn't include the number of cops that are killed each year in the line of duty.

Harassment. Cops face harassment from both directions. They are accused of it, which is simply not true. They also face harassment, they get yelled at, spit at, swore at, called racist and they are threatened amongst many other things. Amazing how many individuals don't want to be harassed at their jobs, but its ok to harass others.

Racism. The trump card of all time. Cops are accused of being racist all the time along with the rest of America and it's not true. Typically, when accusations of racism occur, it's because the offender knows they're guilty and it's their last line of defense. Cops have gotten a bad rap, because certain people and organizations have targeted them for their own personal agendas. It's kind of funny, 99% of the time when someone screams racism, you find out the person was guilty and is a criminal. So, racism had nothing to do with it.

Injustice. Cops are accused of being injustice all the time. That they are not treating someone fair or that their rights are being violated. I'm not sure where along the line when someone decided to commit a crime or to be a criminal, that they thought they still had rights. When you decided to commit a crime, you decided that you didn't care about your rights. As for being treated fairly, you will be in the court of law. Most cops treat people with respect and care about the rights of everyone.

Rejection. Because of a false narrative that is being portrayed about cops, they can't live a normal life. Much of society has shunned cops, because of all the false information. I'm willing to bet that some cops have friends or even family members that don't talk to them anymore, because of the crap that's being portrayed. Nice that society would treat the people that we need the most this way, very unfair.

Sexism. Oh yah, when the race card doesn't work, you might as well call a cop a sexist. I have a hard time believing that when a cop walks up to a car, that the first words out of his mouth are about your sex or your looks. But they get accused of it all the time.

Intolerance. There are people out there that have a short fuse. They have absolutely no tolerance for an officer. They automatically label them as the bad guy, they immediately go on attack. Most encounters between police and individuals start off calm, but not with these individuals. They are like a shark that smells blood, ready to attack. They will automatically start arguing, yelling, or degrading an officer. They don't care what the truth or the facts are, its going to be the cops fault no matter what. They are going to take out all their frustrations on a cop.

Ignorance. I love these people, the uneducated part of society. These are the people that listen to their friends, social media or some news station that has an agenda and portrays false information about cops. Then they buy into it, without educating themselves. Because of their unwillingness to educate themselves, they're going to believe all the falsehoods they've heard. Then they are going to treat the officer unfairly or disrespect them. How would you like someone to tell lies about you at work and everyone believes it. Then they treat you like crap, instead of getting the truth. Doesn't seem fair.

Assaults. There are over 58,000 assaults against law enforcement officers each year. That's around 160 per day. These assaults come in many forms. Most assaults are verbal, but other more serious assaults occur every day. Cops face physical attacks of all kinds. There are numerous times in a day, that cops must draw their weapon to protect themselves. Their most likely isn't a day that goes by, that a cop is forced to protect himself from someone who pulls a gun or knife and tries to kill them. They have no choice but to try to protect themselves and the public.

Injuries. Many cops are injured daily. From minor injuries to more severe injuries. They face an on slot of physical attacks. It can be as simple as cuts and scrapes from altercations, getting hit with weapons or a car, being stabbed with a knife or shot with a weapon. The bottom line is it shouldn't have to be this way, but that's the way society is. Over 160 cops are injured daily, and the number is growing.

Ethics. Most cops have ethics and follow the law. The problem they face Today is there's some people and organizations that have no ethics at all. These people and organizations tell lies and create false narratives for their own agenda. This means that cops face a barrage of attacks daily because false information is being portrayed. How would you feel if you went to work and had to deal with this?

I'm going to talk about ethics a little more because I want to prove a point. As I was compiling some facts for this book, I decided to do some searching on the net. My quest was to find out how many officers have been injured or killed while on duty. No matter how I changed the wording it took me 20 searches to come up with the info. Every time that search engine took me to people that have been shot by cops. I never once asked for that information.

Why did it take me to that information? Because they have a narrative and an agenda to push. Their goal is to make cops look like the bad people. That cops are racist and shoot certain people. They have manipulated their search engine and news stories to fit their agenda. They don't want you to know what the truth is. So, they are manipulating you into reading what they want, to push their agenda.

Rights. Yes, cops have rights too. But it seems that their rights don't matter. Right now, cops' rights are under attack for the wrong reasons. There's people and organizations that are attacking their rights, for their own personal agendas. I not sure when society decided criminals had rights, but cops don't. Doesn't seem fair.

Other Hazards Cops Face

Police officers run a high risk of being attacked, wounded, or even killed by criminals and other people whose behavior disagrees with the law and the society norms.

Many police officers are involved in work-related accidents - vehicle crashes, falls during chase, rescue, and similar operations, etc. Slips, trips, and falls while chasing suspects in a crime.

Police officers usually live under constant apprehension of physical danger, work long and irregular hours, and are exposed to unpleasant sides of life. This often results in psychological stress, family, and personal problems.

Police officers may develop health problems because of spending much time outdoors, including under the sun or in bad weather. They also have health issues due to stress from the job.

Unavoidable physical contact with people who have contagious diseases is a serious health hazard.

Accidents are most likely during emergency response of the policeman and may occur especially while doing first aid work, patrol car driving and riot control.

Wounds caused by knife or other object because of being attacked by persons contacted in the course of duty. Wounds caused by random or careless shooting by others.

Post-traumatic stress disorder (PTSD), most likely if the incident witnessed by the policeman has resulted in serious injury, or death to any of those involved.

Fear of being prosecuted afterward for actions which seemed to be clearly indicated as necessary during an event, but later not considered as such particularly by others.

The paperwork duties, as opposed to active law enforcement, are often experienced as a major stressor.

Bad Neighborhoods & Cities

Whether you want to believe it or not, there are some bad neighborhoods in America. The crime rate in these neighborhoods is astronomically high. There are also cities across America, where the crime rate is out of control.

I'm not going to list them. You can look them up if you're interested. What I do know is that the crime rate has reached all-time highs in many of these areas. The crime rate is rising daily, and it looks like it's going to get way worse as time goes on.

The crimes that are committed in these areas are some of the worst. Many people are stabbed and shot daily. The gun violence in these areas is out of control. I think everyone in America is aware that we have an issue.

The reason I'm bringing this up in this book is, because I have some questions for you. Are you willing to deal with it? Are you willing to get stabbed or shot at to help make these neighborhoods safe?

How would you like to go to work today in one of these neighborhoods, knowing that most likely you will be assaulted, stabbed, or shot at?

This is what cops must face every day when they work in these neighborhoods or cities. They have an 80% chance that when they respond to a call in one of these areas, that there will be a weapon involved. They will be harassed, assaulted, stabbed, or shot at.

Police officers live under constant apprehension of physical danger in these areas, work long and irregular hours. They are exposed to the worst that society has to offer. This often results in psychological stress, family, and personal problems.

Yet, the only people trying to keep these areas safe, are the cops. Then some of society disrespects them and treats them like they are the bad guys. Not to mention they want to reform, defund, or dismantle cops. Makes absolutely no sense.

The only action we need in this country, is keeping the criminals off the streets. We need to stop letting criminals out of jail, so the communities will be safe. We need more cops, with stricter laws.

Society has no one to blame for the rise in crime, but themselves. That's right, all this talk about police reform, defunding and dismantling the police, has helped raise the crime rate. Here's why.

Cops are tired of being treated badly. A lot of cops decided to retire early or quit the force from all the harassment and stress. Cops have decided to take jobs in areas where they are treated better and there's less crime. This leaves less cops in your neighborhood. Less cops equals higher crime.

No one is going to sign up to be a cop in your area, because of the way they are treated and the high crime rate. This means less cops to uphold the law. Which means more crime.

What did you think was going to happen? Did you

think all the criminals in your neighborhood would stop doing crimes once the police disappeared? That you were all going to join hands, and life would be a basket full of roses. Heck no, the criminals just got an open door to do more crimes and run your neighborhood with no one to stop them.

Not to mention, there will be more poverty and no jobs in these communities. The people and businesses that can leave, will. Many businesses will close. Housing values will drop due to the high crime. Banks will not give loans to businesses which will hurt the community.

So, for all the people who thought that police reform, defunding or dismantling the police was a brilliant idea. Don't whine and complain when businesses close or the criminals come knocking at your door. You got what you asked for, less cops, higher crime, be happy.

As for all the great citizens in these areas and there are a lot of great citizens in every community. I feel bad for you because you will be affected by all this. But you're not off the hook completely. This is what happens when you allow a few people in your community or organizations that have their own personal agenda. To voice their opinions and you don't put an end to it and stand up for what's right for the majority of the good hard-working people.

For the rest of America who may not be affected by this right now. You will be eventually if all this rhetoric keeps up. The more areas they do police reform or defunding in, will have less cops and you experience high crime. Crime has no boundaries and eventually spreads across America.

Officer Down

Being a law enforcement officer is no easy job. Where else do you leave for work knowing you may have to put your life on the line that day. There have been over 22,000 officers killed in the line of duty.

Officers face the reality that on average 1 officer is killed every 58 hours. Let's not forget about the constant onslaught of assaults. On average there are over 58,000 assaults on law enforcement officers each year. That's about 160 per day.

Below is a list of yearly recorded numbers for police officers that have died while on duty for a 10-year period.

    2010 - 180 police officers died in the line of duty
    2011 - 187 police officers died in the line of duty
    2012 - 141 police officers died in the line of duty
    2013 - 128 police officers died in the line of duty
    2014 - 158 police officers died in the line of duty
    2015 - 164 police officers died in the line of duty
    2016 - 171 police officers died in the line of duty
    2017 - 152 police officers died in the line of duty
    2018 - 150 police officers died in the line of duty
    2019 - 150 police officers died in the line of duty

Officer Down

2020 - 362 police officers died in the line of duty

As you can see, 2020 was the deadliest year for police. The number of officers who died while in the line of duty more than doubled in one year.

2021 is starting off with the same results. The first 100 days of 2021, 1 officer has died per day. If that keeps up, it will be the second highest year or may surpass 2020. Nationwide, 117 law enforcement officers have lost their lives in the first four months of 2021

There have been more than 22,000 law enforcement officers killed in the line of duty. Currently, there are 22,611 names engraved on the walls of the National Law Enforcement Officers Memorial. There are over 2000 federal officers listed on the Memorial. There are 393 female officers listed on the Memorial. The names of the 394 fallen officers who have been added in 2020 to the wall.

A total of 1,943 law enforcement officers died in the line of duty during the past 10 years, an average of 194 per year. There were 362 law enforcement officers who died in the line of duty in 2020. The deadliest year in law enforcement history was 2020, when 362 officers died in the line of duty.

There are over 58,000 assaults against law enforcement officers each year. That's around 160 per day. How would you like to work under these conditions? Knowing when you go to work, you will most likely be assaulted.

The deadliest day in law enforcement history was September 11, 2001, when 72 officers were killed while responding to the terrorist attacks on America. They risked their lives and put themselves in harm's way to help other people.

The New York City Police Department has lost more officers in the line of duty than any other department. Texas has lost more officers, than any other state.

2020 was one of the deadliest years for law enforcement officers in the history of the United States. 362 law enforcement officers died in the line of duty in 2020 representing a 96% increase compared to the previous year. 24 female officers died in 2020

In 2021 the first 100 days of the year, there were over 100 cops killed, that's one or more a day. This doesn't include cops that were shot and injured, who didn't pass away from their injuries? It also doesn't include the number of assaults that take place daily. Which is around 160 per day.

Now that you've had a look at what cop's face while on duty. How would you like to face this every day when you go to work? Better yet, how would you like to be a cop and live in their shoes.

Racial Tensions

I was going to try and stay away from talking about race or racism in this book. But, because it seems to be one of the biggest topics in our society, I figure we better cover it. Right now, cops are being blamed for racism and its simply not true.

Right now, in the United States we already have an issue with racial tension. It has gotten worse over the past several years. The division in our country has grown. Not due to the good American people, we have other forces inciting it.

I never understood it myself. I don't wake up in the morning with hatred toward someone else. I don't blame other people for my problems. I just go about my life like normal and it's the last thing that ever crosses my mind.

I believe that most Americans are the same, they just go about their lives. Most Americans are not racist. Most Americans are very generous and will give you the shirt off their back. Americans are one of largest groups of people that donate to just about every cause. Not only in America, but globally.

When there's a crisis in the United States, most Americans stand up and help. They help in multiple ways, monetarily and many show up in person. America has the largest number of people willing to volunteer.

Every time there's a crisis in America the people show up in numbers to help. Whether they are cleaning up, rebuilding, supplying food or water. They give their blood, sweat and tears to help. It doesn't matter what color, race, or religion the person is that they're helping, they show up. This action proves that most Americans are not racist and will help anyone that needs it.

The problem we have in America is, there's small groups of people and a few organizations that want to portray that we have a bigger issue with racism and it's not true. They want to portray that America itself is racist and that's far from the truth. They are trying to force feed it to everyone else for their own personal agendas.

It seems that there are certain groups of people and organizations that are prone to forcing racial tensions onto the rest of us. It seems that it's the only way they know how to deal with issues or to push their own personal agendas.

Let's talk about groups and organizations pushing their own personal agendas. When George Floyd died, I'm sure there was some people that were upset or affected by this. I don't want to take anything away from that or diminish that fact.

But there were groups and organizations that used it as a tool to raise racial tensions in our country and pour fuel onto the fire for their own personal agendas. We had certain groups and organizations that invoked chaos and rioting in our streets for their own personal agendas.

They didn't care one bit about George Floyd or what happened to him. That's the truth. They just needed an excuse to push their own personal agenda and they used George Floyd for it. They were just waiting for an excuse and jumped into action.

The problem is these groups and organizations

did a lot of damage to good neighborhoods. By invoking rioting, luting, and burning down many good hard working Americans things. They created chaos for all of us. These organizations and groups are still using it as their excuse to push their own personal agendas.

Before I move on. I want to say that I believe black lives do matter, I believe all lives matter. I think many people are aware that these groups and organizations used everyone else to push their own personal agendas and that's not fair to everyone else. They invoked chaos and that was not most people's agenda.

They also took away your right to protest peacefully, voice your concerns and be heard, that's not fair. I believe that people do have a right to protest peacefully when issues arrive. But, when you have groups and organizations inciting riots for their own personal agenda, it doesn't help anyone. Especially when they really don't care about what the real issue is. That's not fair for everyone else involved or who did care.

I never understood why some people want to blame others for their issues. Many Americans have issues. They get up in the morning and look in the mirror and try to figure out a solution to the problem. They don't run around blaming someone else.

Running around all day blaming someone else or being agitated does no good. It turns you into a miserable person. Then you just start living a miserable life and make everyone around you miserable. Doesn't sound like much fun.

At the time I'm writing this we have 382 million people in the United states. We have a few thousand people and a few organizations that are causing issues. It's a small percentage compared to the total population.

As you can see, with such a large population, it's only a few people or organizations that are pushing their agenda. We don't have an overall problem with racism, not like they want us to believe. Most Americans are great people and don't care about race at all. There's not an issue with systemic racism like they want you to believe.

Here's the problem we face in America. The more we allow these groups and organizations to affect our opinions or beliefs, the more people will start believing it's true. The more people that are swayed into believing it's true, will create more racial tensions among everybody.

The more racial tensions that are created, will create more problems between all of us. The next thing you know we will have a bigger problem than what really exists. This is not a good scenario and doesn't need to happen. It will not be good for any of us and will lead to major problems in the future.

What we need to do is turn off and ignore all the negative energy that is being force fed to us, even by these organizations. Their only mission is to turn all of us against each other, so they can say, see we do have a problem. Then they will use it for their own personal agenda. We must find a way to put an end to this.

It's time that America comes together and stop these people that are trying to divide us. The division that they're creating is not good for America and will only lead to more racial tensions. Their plan to tear everyone apart for their own personal agendas, needs to stop.

It's time for us to stand up and stop with the social media garbage. Turn off the news sources that are portraying America as a systemically racist country, cause it's not true. Time for us to tell our government to stop with their personal agenda of tearing America apart, so they can rebuild it and take control of your life.

If we don't learn to tune out all the negative forces, the future of the United states will not be a genuinely nice place to live. We will all be pitted against each other and we will have racial wars amongst our own people. I think most of us don't want to see that happen. It's time we start focusing on positive energy and focus on making America a great place to live, for everyone.

Lastly, you are being used and manipulated for others personal agendas. America doesn't have a systemic racism problem. Americans are some of the greatest people on this planet. Please don't be fooled by their personal agendas.

One last thing, you need to stop blaming the cops. Most cops are normal hard-working people and are not racist. These groups and organizations are painting a false narrative to push their agenda and they are targeting cops to make that happen. When it's not the cops that are creating the problem. You're being used and lied too.

Cops no Cops

Well, the issue of whether we should have police or not, is becoming a big topic in America. It's creating a lot of controversy.

Many people call this defunding the police or dismantling the police altogether. I'm positive that not having police, will be bad for society.

I'm not sure where most of the population benefits from not having police. Yet we have certain people and organizations pushing to get rid of police. There main goal is to make the police look like the bad guys and in 99% of the cases, it's not true. They have their own personal agendas, and they are targeting cops to get it done.

The problem you have is every time there's a police shooting in America, you don't get all the facts. There's many people and organizations out there that are exploiting these shootings for their own personal agenda. They don't care one bit about the individual who was shot, all they care about is their agenda. They are using Americans as a pawn in their chess game.

Now, as usual, I like to give examples. On 4/12/21 a kid by the name of Daunte Wright was shot and

Officer Down

killed during a traffic stop. I want you to watch the video of this incident. Just type in Daunte Wright Brooklyn Center MN Body Cam. It will show everything that happens, but I will run through the course of events and give you a real look.

The kid is pulled over for having expired tabs on his vehicle, legitimate reason. Everything starts out as a normal traffic stop. What you don't know, but the cops do know, is he has warrant out for his arrest. The warrant is for multiple weapon charges.

It looks like a normal traffic stop. The cops approach the car in a normal manner and ask the kid to get out of the car. The kid complies and all is going well. At some point during the time that the officer is trying to put handcuffs on the kid decides he doesn't want to comply anymore.

He wrestles himself away from the cop and jumps back in his car in an attempt, to flee. This is where the chaos starts. He is accidently shot by an officer who thought she had her taser, instead of her firearm. The outcome is a tragedy, I don't want to take anything away from that, but I will make my point.

If the kid would have complied, the shooting would have never happened. His actions made the rest of this scenario play out in a bad way. He put everyone in a bad spot, his actions caused this to happen. If he would have just complied, he would still be alive. That's a fact.

Now the other fact is this. He had a warrant out for his arrest. This means that he decided not to go to court and face whatever he was charged for. He made the decision to avoid dealing with it. Then when the cops do catch up to him and it's time to deal with it, he decides once again to flee the scene.

If he would have dealt with it right away, no one would have been put in this spot. Yet you want to blame the cops, because he didn't take care of it when he should have. There must be some ownership here.

I want you to look at it this way. If he would have taken care of the issue up-front. There wouldn't have been a warrant for his arrest. Then none of this would have happened. He decided not to take care of it and that's why there was a warrant for his arrest.

Let's talk about Makhia Bryant. She is a girl that was shot by a cop, while she was trying to stab another girl. Almost Immediately some people and organizations start yelling racism.

There is nothing in either one of these videos that indicates any racism at all. When you watch the Makhia Bryant video, make sure you watch both the cop cam and the neighbors garage video.

The cop has literally seconds to react to a chaotic scene. She tries to stab another girl and she is going to stab the girl in pink and the cop makes the right decision to defend that girl's life.

I don't think that in the few seconds this cop had to react to a girl on a rampage trying to stab other people, that race even entered his mind. He reacted to the situation and that's all. Not a racist issue.

It's tough being honest isn't it. In both these

cases, the perpetrator determines the outcome. If you comply, you don't get shot. If you own up to and face what you need too and take care of your business, you don't get shot. If you don't run around with a knife and try to stab someone you live.

Now, I was going to try to stay away from talking about George Floyd, but I must address it. Why, because it sparked one of the biggest uproars in our country. I think we all agree that the way that George died on that day was not right. It was uncalled for, I'm with everyone on that. I just want everyone to understand that.

But here's where I think a lot of people have an issue. George Floyd was not a role model citizen. He had a rap sheet the length of his arm. Yet everyone is trying to portray him as a great citizen, pillar of the community.

Role model citizens don't commit crimes against other people. They surely don't threaten people's lives with a gun, look up his arrest sheet. On the day of his incident, he was committing another crime. If he were a role model citizen like the rest of us, he would have been at home baking cookies, not drugs.

My point is, none of this happens if George Floyd is a role model citizen. His actions of being a career criminal and doing another crime, is what causes all this to happen. The cops would have had no reason to be there. His criminal activities brought all this on. The result was tragic, but he created it by being a criminal.

The truth hurts don't it. When you get right to the bottom of it, his way of life of being a criminal and his actions caused all of it. If he would have ran his life like a role model citizen, he wouldn't have put anyone in that situation.

Some of society needs a reality check. The very minute that you take a criminal and you turn him into a national hero. We have some real issues in America that need to be addressed. If you think George Floyd is a hero, you've got some rethinking to do. A real hero is a cop that puts his life on the line to protect society and your neighborhood from criminals.

I realize that a lot of Americans are smart enough to dig into the facts, before they make a rash decision and start blaming the cops. But we have some people that just want to fly off the handle, start yelling, screaming, and acting out right away. Without knowing all the facts.

Try educating yourself first before flying off the handle. Stop buying into the crap on social media. I think you will discover that the people that the cops are trying to get off our streets, are not good for our society. We have a lot of great people in our society and most of us just want to live a peaceful life. We don't want criminals running our streets and controlling our neighborhoods.

By the way, stop yelling racism every time one of these shootings or incidents happen. Get the facts, there's more white people killed during police shootings than blacks. It's more than double. So, it's not a race issue and many cops are not racist. We don't have a systemic race issue like certain people and organizations want you to believe.

There's more black-on-black shootings than any other shootings, but nobody's complaining about that. Yet every time a cop shoots a black person who is most likely a criminal or committing a crime, it becomes a big deal. Most shootings in black neighborhoods are done by black people and there's no issue here. Nobody wants to talk about that. 95% of blacks killed are killed by black people.

Doesn't make sense. It appears to me you might want more cops in your neighborhood to help deal with this, so you can live in peace. No one is talking about what's happening in your neighborhood, why not. Why aren't we addressing the real issues. The crime in your community. We're not dealing with the real issue, instead we're trying to blame everyone else. When the real issue is in your own community.

20 blacks are killed every day in this country by the violence happening in their own neighborhoods, by their own people. Not one word is mentioned or are the real issues being dealt with. Everyone is ignoring the real issue and trying to use the race card to push their own personal agendas.

We need to deal with the real issues, so you can have a nice neighborhood to live in. Stop the government and other organizations from using blacks, black crime, or police shootings for their own personal agenda. Get them to deal with the real issue and that is making your community a better place to live.

Let me bring up one more point and I want you to think about this. Did you know that during a criminal's career, at some point he will escalate to extremely bad violence? This means that at some point he's going to hurt or kill someone.

I hope it's not you, your family, or kids that experience this. Because you made the decision to defund or dismantle the police. Someone must remove the criminals before this happens. If you defund or dismantle the police, many people will experience the wrath of criminals.

Police reform. I'm sure that police can learn or use new techniques. But what's being portrayed to America is some people don't want cops to carry guns. So, you're trying to tell us that it's ok for criminals to carry guns, but cops should not. So, your good with criminals running around and shooting up your neighborhood. When you call a cop to respond, that doesn't have a gun, how's that going to work out for you.

You're also telling us that a criminal has a right to protect his life, but a cop doesn't. Let's think about this. Most cops are hardworking average American citizens, that took a vow to protect society from thugs, thieves, and criminals. You're saying that a cop's life is worth less than a criminal's life. You want cops to get shot and killed with no way to defend themselves from the criminals that they're trying to protect you from.

Officer Down

This makes no sense at all.

I've got a plan, check this out. I say we hire way more cops, give them as many guns as they need. Get the military involved and they go out and round up every criminal in America. Ship them to a deserted island somewhere. Then the rest of us can live in peace without all this chaos.

Now let me ask you a question. Do you think cops get up in the morning and say, I'm going to go out and shoot someone Today? Do you think they get up with the attitude they want to go out and confront, thugs, thieves, and criminals every day? Do you think they enjoy dealing with criminals?

I doubt it, most cops are average citizens. They would love nothing more than to go to work and have a nice peaceful quite day like the rest of us at our jobs. But every society breeds criminals. Someone must deal with the criminals. If you want to do it yourself, then defund or dismantle the police and you will get your chance.

Defunding or getting rid of the police is the worst thing you could do for society; it puts everyone at risk. The thugs, thieves and criminals will own your neighborhood. They will be knocking down your door to get what you have. They will own you and take whatever dignity you have left.

You might want to buy a gun because you will have to defend yourself. You could call 911, but nobody's there, so you are left to defend yourself and your family. You just signed up to be cop by defunding or dismantling the police.

Now that you have the attitude that defunding the police was a great thing, let me give you some information on what police officers must face. It is April 14th of 2021 and this year over 100 cops have been shot and died while on duty. That's about 1 cop a day getting shot and dying. How would you like to go to work and deal with that? Like I said, defund or dismantle the police and you will get the opportunity.

The odds of you experiencing a criminal at your door will increase drastically, because the only thing keeping the criminals from knocking your door down right now is the police. Get rid of the police and you will get an opportunity to have criminals knocking down your door. I'm not sure about you, but I would rather have a cop knocking on my door, not a criminal.

If you defund police or dismantle the police, the criminals will be running society. It will be total chaos. You will not be able to go anywhere because you will be confronted by thugs, thieves, and criminals. The streets and neighborhoods will not be safe. Your kids will not be able to go to school because the gang members will rule them. Your kids will not be able to go outside because gangs will be controlling every neighborhood.

There will be many innocent people getting attacked and shot, because that's how gang members deal with things. The United States will revert to the wild, wild west. Everyone will be carrying a gun and it will look like a shootout at the ok corral.

Bottom line is, it will not be safe to go anywhere or do anything. By defunding or dismantling cops, you just signed away your right to be free. You'll no longer have the freedom to go anywhere or do anything.

To live in a society where we can have freedom, we must have laws. The laws must be enforced, and someone must enforce them. Without laws, society turns into total chaos. You can't live in a society without laws. The minute you remove laws, society is taken over by thugs, thieves, and criminals.

By now there's a couple things running through your mind while you're reading this. Because I'm so adamant about not defunding the police. You're thinking I'm a cop, the answer is no. I just know what's going to happen to society if you have no police. The outcome is detrimental for all of us and I'm not alone in my decision not to defund police.

85% of Americans that were polled, said they don't want the police to be defunded. The poll showed they want more police. A poll that was done among black citizens showed that 80% didn't believe in defunding the police. That they wanted police in their communities and more of a police presence.

I stand with the majority of America. I believe we need police. Since 85% of all Americans believe in having more police, then why are we even talking about defunding police.

You have certain people and organizations that are using it for their own personal agendas. They are adding fuel to the fire for their personal gain. They are also trying to use it to raise racial tensions in America, to help fulfill their own personal agenda. They're advocating this and using the people as their guinea pigs. You're being lied to and used for other people's personal agendas.

As for the rioting on the streets, you may have some gang members that would love nothing more than to have the police removed from their neighborhood. We know what their agenda is, to own and run your neighborhoods. This will not turnout out to be good thing for all the great citizens of this country.

Since the government knows most of the population does not agree with what's happening, why aren't they taking action to stop the rioting. Because they have their own personal agenda.

What it does show, is they don't care about what the majority of America wants. All they care about is their own personal agendas and it proves they don't care about America as a whole. If they did, they would put an end to this nonsense, instead of supporting it.

There's 380 million people in the US. There's a few thousand people that are disrupting our lives and it must come to an end. It's time for the rest of America too voice our opinions and let them know, we don't agree with how they're handling this. They need to stop catering to these small groups, organizations and do what's right for the majority.

It's time we let them know, to get these people off

our streets. So, the rest of us can live in peace. There's plenty of great people in every neighborhood in America and we all want to live in peace, and go on with our lives, we're tired of the rhetoric.

Oh, if you live somewhere that is not affected by all this chaos, if the police are defunded, it will reach your area. Criminals have no boundaries, eventually they will spread across the country like a plague. The only cure for this disease will be a gun. If we don't put an end to this now, the future of the US will be an all-out war. Anarchy will reign across America.

Lastly, the government has a plan to remove cops from the streets and go to military policing. They will not be doing this to protect you, it will be done to control you. Why do you think they are releasing criminals back onto our streets? One more point. Why is the government, whether its federal or local releasing criminals back onto the streets?

They want total anarchy, so they can step in and take over. They are using everything they can from allowing the riots to continue, releasing criminals, racism, and defunding police to push their agenda.

They're instituting chaos in your neighborhoods, so when they must step in, they will try to look like heroes. Behind the scenes they have a hidden agenda and that's all about controlling America. You're being deceived into falling for it and believing that they have your best interest in mind. It's a huge smoke screen, don't fall for it. They have a plan to control every aspect of your life.

Dialing 911

Here's what's funny about people. They want to disgrace, assault and attack cops. They want police reform, defunding or dismantling of the police. They want to blame cops for issues like racism that aren't their fault and aren't true.

Some of America has taken attacks against anyone involved in law enforcement. You asked for less police involvement in your area, and you got it.

When a crime is taking place or you need a cop, the first thing you do is dial 911. The problem is no one responds, or their response time is slow. Why is no one responding.

It's not that the cops don't want to do their job and respond. It's because there's not enough cops left to respond. You got what you asked for.

Because of the attacks on police officers. Many police officers decided to retire early or quit their jobs. They left the force. Many officers decided to leave the departments they were in and take jobs where they are treated better or don't have to deal with all the rhetoric.

That's right, you got what you asked for. Here's an example. In Minneapolis they lost 200 cops from the force. Many officers retired, quit, or moved on to better areas where they don't have to deal with all this rhetoric and attacks.

So, if you dial 911 and can't get a cop to respond fast enough, it's your fault. Because of your actions and the way, you treated police. There are now less cops in your area. Less cops equals higher crime.

What did you think was going to happen? Did you think the police were just going to put up with all this harassment? No one wants to put up with that kind of scrutiny. Most of us would do the same thing if that's how we got treated at our jobs. If I were a cop, I would leave, I wouldn't put up with it.

People make absolutely no sense. Now you want to turn around and blame the cops for not responding fast enough when there's a crime. You want to yell and scream that you need a cop now. You now want to blame the cops because they're not there when you need them.

Too funny, you took the time to attack cops and told them you didn't want them or their protection. Now the criminals are running your neighborhoods and the crime rate is skyrocketing. Now you want cops. Makes absolutely no sense and many people knew this was going to happen.

You can't have it both ways. Either you make a choice to have police and live under laws, so your community can be safe. Or you choose to have no police and let the criminals run your neighborhoods. We all see how that's working out.

As for all the great citizens in these areas where the crime is skyrocketing, I feel bad for you. But like I said before, you're not completely of the hook. This is what happens when you allow a few people to make decisions for your community. You should have gone out and stood up for the cops and put an end to all this rhetoric.

The bad part about this whole deal is many good people are going to be affected by the criminals that are now overtaking your communities. There's going to be a lot of innocent blood spilled, because you decided not to protect the police.

But remember if you dial 911 and need a cop to respond and they don't show up. It's not their fault. They did respond by doing what you asked them to do. They resigned, quit, or moved on, exactly what you asked for. So, no ones left to protect you.

Conclusion

The police have an incredibly hard job, and believe me, I know there are violent people that harm the community and police but that's not all of us. We must acknowledge that it's not working, and we must get together to come up with a solution. It's urgent that we come up with a solution because the crime rate is sky rocketing.

The bottom line is no one should have to go to work and put up with being harassed, attacked, assaulted, or shot at. It appears that we need to treat officers with more respect and have their back. With all they must deal with to keep our communities safe, it's not an easy job.

What I do know is that allowing criminals to run our communities will not be a good. To live in a good society, we must have laws. Without laws, there is total chaos. There needs to be people to uphold the laws and that's why we need cops.

Author Information

Thanks for taking time to read my book. If you read this book, please check one of my America's Future Books. I think you will be amazed at what the future of America has coming.

If you have any input or topics, you want me to discuss in my books. You can contact me at.

billygrinslott@gmail.com

Please help by spreading the word about this book. I would be greatly appreciated.

If you could take the time to give me a good review. It would be greatly appreciated.

Website – billygrinslott.com

Thanks. Billy Grinslott

Copyright © 2021. All rights reserved.

Officer Down

Officer Down

www.ingramcontent.com/pod-product-compliance
Lightning Source LLC
Chambersburg PA
CBHW070825220526
45466CB00002B/759